SACREDSPACE

for Lent 2007

SACREDSPACE

for Lent 2007

from the web site www.sacredspace.ie
Jesuit Communication Centre, Ireland

ave maria press **AmP** notre dame, indiana

Acknowledgment

The publisher would like to thank Gerry Bourke SJ and Alan McGuckian SJ for their kind assistance in making this book possible. Gerry Bourke SJ can be contacted on feedback@jesuit.ie

Unless otherwise noted, the Scripture quotations contained herein are from the *New Revised Standard Version Bible*, copyright © 1989 by the Division of Christian Education of the National Council of the Churches of Christ in the United States of America. Used by permission. All rights reserved.

Published under license from Michelle Anderson Publishing Pty. Ltd. in Australia.

Founded in 1865, Ave Maria Press is a ministry of the Indiana Province of Holy Cross.

www.avemariapress.com

ISBN-10 1-59471-121-6   ISBN-13 978-1-59471-121-3

Cover and text design by K.H. Coney

Printed and bound in the United States of America.

how to use this book

During this Lenten season, we invite you to make a sacred space in your day. Spend ten minutes praying here and now, wherever you are, with the help of a prayer guide and scripture chosen specially for each day. Every place is a sacred space so you may wish to have this little book available at any time or place during the course of the day . . . in your desk at work, while traveling, on your bedside table, in your purse or jacket pocket. . . . Remember that God is everywhere, all around us, constantly reaching out to us, even in the most unlikely situations. When we know this, and with a bit of practice, we can pray anywhere.

The following pages will guide you through a session of prayer stages.

Something to think and pray about each day this week
The Presence of God
Freedom
Consciousness
The Word (leads you to the daily Lenten scripture and provides help with the text)
Conversation
Conclusion

It is most important to come back to these pages each day of the week as they are an integral part of each day's prayer and lead to the scripture and inspiration points.

Although written in the first person the prayers are for "doing" rather than for reading out. Each stage is a kind of exercise or mediation aimed at helping you to get in touch with God and God's presence in your life.

We hope that you will join the many people around the world praying with us in our sacred space.

The Presence of God

Bless all who worship you, almighty God,
from the rising of the sun to its setting:
from your goodness enrich us,
by your love inspire us,
by your Spirit guide us,
by your power protect us,
in your mercy receive us,
now and always.

Something to think and pray about each day this week:

Getting started

We are starting Lent this week, a somber time. You did not come, O God, to judge us, but to seek what is lost, to set free those who are imprisoned in guilt and fear, and to save us when our hearts accuse us.

Take us as we are here with all that sinful past of the world. You are greater than our heart, and greater than all our guilt—you are the creator of a new future and a God of Love for ever and ever.

The Presence of God

I pause for a moment and think of the love and the grace that God showers on me, creating me in his image and likeness, making me his temple.

Freedom

Everything has the potential to draw forth from me a fuller love and life.
Yet my desires are often fixed, caught, on illusions of fulfillment.
I ask that God, through my freedom, may orchestrate
my desires in a vibrant loving melody rich in harmony.

Consciousness

In the presence of my loving Creator,
I look honestly at my feelings over the last day, the highs, the lows and the level ground. Can I see where the Lord has been present?

The Word

God speaks to each one of us individually. I need to listen to what he is saying to me. (Please turn to your scripture on the following pages. Inspiration points are there should you need them. When you are ready, return here to continue.)

Conversation

What feelings are rising in me
as I pray and reflect on God's Word?
I imagine Jesus himself sitting or standing beside me, and open my heart to him.

Conclusion

Glory be to the Father, and to the Son, and to the Holy Spirit,
As it was in the beginning, is now and ever shall be,
World without end. Amen

Wednesday 21st February
Ash Wednesday   Joel 2:12–14

Yet even now, says the Lord, return to me with all your heart, with fasting, with weeping, and with mourning; rend your hearts and not your clothing. Return to the Lord, your God, for he is gracious and merciful, slow to anger, and abounding in steadfast love, and relents from punishing. Who knows whether he will not turn and relent, and leave a blessing behind him, a grain offering and a drink offering for the Lord, your God?

- "Return to me with all your heart . . . rend your hearts and not your clothing." The Lord asks not for a list of good deeds but for a profound revolution within us.

- Perhaps I can start from Joel's description of the Lord's character—graciousness, mercy, slowness to anger, steadfastness, love. . . .

Thursday 22nd February
The See of St. Peter Matthew 16:13–19

Now when Jesus came into the district of Caesarea Philippi, he asked his disciples, "Who do people say that the Son of Man is?" And they said, "Some say John the Baptist, but others Elijah, and still others Jeremiah or one of the prophets." He said to them, "But who do you say that I am?" Simon Peter answered, "You are the Messiah, the Son of the living God." And Jesus answered him, "Blessed are you, Simon son of Jonah! For flesh and blood has not revealed this to you, but my Father in heaven. And I tell you, you are Peter, and on this rock I will build my church, and the gates of Hades will not prevail against it. I will give you the keys of the kingdom of heaven, and whatever you bind on earth will be bound in heaven, and whatever you loose on earth will be loosed in heaven."

- Peter shows a deeper insight into Jesus than others: He is a prophet, yes, and also the Messiah—but much more too, as Peter recognizes that Jesus has an intimate relationship with God.

- Can I stand alongside Peter? Can I imagine his response to Jesus' answer: "Blessed are you, Simon."?

- On what paths will this God-given insight take him? Or me?

Friday 23rd February   Isaiah 58:5–9

Is such the fast that I choose, a day to humble oneself? Is it to bow down the head like a bulrush, and to lie in sackcloth and ashes? Will you call this a fast, a day acceptable to the Lord? Is not this the fast that I choose: to loose the bonds of injustice, to undo the thongs of the yoke, to let the oppressed go free, and to break every yoke? Is it not to share your bread with the hungry, and bring the homeless poor into your house; when you see the naked, to cover them, and not to hide yourself from your own kin? Then your light shall break forth like the dawn, and your healing shall spring up quickly; your vindicator shall go before you, the glory of the Lord shall be your rear guard. Then you shall call, and the Lord will answer; you shall cry for help, and he will say, Here I am.

- "Is not this the fast that I choose," says the Lord, ". . . to share your bread with the hungry, and bring the homeless poor into your house? . . . Then you shall call and the Lord will answer."

Saturday 24th February   Luke 5:27–32

After this he went out and saw a tax collector named Levi, sitting at the tax booth; and he said to him, "Follow me." And he got up, left everything, and followed him. Then Levi gave a great banquet for him in his house; and there was a large crowd of tax collectors and others sitting at the table with them. The Pharisees and their scribes were complaining to his disciples, saying, "Why do you eat and drink with tax collectors and sinners?" Jesus answered, "Those who are well have no need of a physician, but those who are sick; I have come to call not the righteous but sinners to repentance."

- Levi's response frees him to leave everything and follow.

- Jesus provokes us, as he provokes the religious leaders. Does this letting-go, this repentance, bring joy into my life?

february 25 – march 3

Something to think and pray about each day this week:

Temptations

Father, you are not happy with us when we make each other unhappy. You cannot bear it when we kill and destroy each other. Break, we pray you, the cycle of evil that holds us captive, and let sin die in us, as the sin of the world died in Jesus your son, and death was killed. He lives for us today and every day.

The Presence of God

I reflect for a moment on God's presence around me and in me. Creator of the universe, the sun and the moon, the earth, every molecule, every atom, everything that is: God is in every beat of my heart. God is with me, now.

Freedom

If God were trying to tell me something, would I know? If God were reassuring me or challenging me, would I notice? I ask for the grace to be free of my own preoccupations and open to what God may be saying to me.

Consciousness

How do I find myself today?
Where am I with God? With others?
Do I have something to be grateful for? Then I give thanks.
Is there something I am sorry for? Then I ask forgiveness.

The Word

I read the Word of God slowly, a few times over, and I listen to what God is saying to me. (Please turn to your scripture on the following pages. Inspiration points are there should you need them. When you are ready, return here to continue.)

Conversation

What is stirring in me as I pray?
Am I consoled, troubled, left cold?
I imagine Jesus himself standing or sitting at my side,
and share my feelings with him.

Conclusion

Glory be to the Father, and to the Son, and to the Holy Spirit,
As it was in the beginning, is now and ever shall be,
World without end. Amen

Sunday 25th February
First Sunday of Lent   Luke 4:1–13

Jesus, full of the Holy Spirit, returned from the Jordan and was led by the Spirit in the wilderness, where for forty days he was tempted by the devil. He ate nothing at all during those days, and when they were over, he was famished. The devil said to him, "If you are the Son of God, command this stone to become a loaf of bread." Jesus answered him, "It is written, 'One does not live by bread alone.'" Then the devil led him up and showed him in an instant all the kingdoms of the world. And the devil said to him, "To you I will give their glory and all this authority; for it has been given over to me, and I give it to anyone I please. If you, then, will worship me, it will all be yours." Jesus answered him, "It is written, 'Worship the Lord your God, and serve only him.'" Then the devil took him to Jerusalem, and placed him on the pinnacle of the temple, saying to him, "If you are the Son of God, throw yourself down from here, for it is written, 'He will command his angels concerning you, to protect you,' and 'On their hands they will bear you up, so that you will not dash your foot against a stone.'" Jesus answered him, "It is said, 'Do not put the Lord your God to the test.'" When the devil had finished every test, he departed from him until an opportune time.

- How do the temptations of Jesus speak to my life? Do the devil's false promises and manipulations ring a bell with me?

- How am I tempted to dominate and use the material gifts of the world around me?

- Does the realization of temptation in my life weigh me down?

Monday 26th February
Matthew 25:31–40

"When the Son of Man comes in his glory, and all the angels with him, then he will sit on the throne of his glory. All the nations will be gathered before him, and he will separate people one from another as a shepherd separates the sheep from the goats, and he will put the sheep at his right hand and the goats at the left. Then the king will say to those at his right hand, 'Come, you that are blessed by my Father, inherit the kingdom prepared for you from the foundation of the world; for I was hungry and you gave me food, I was thirsty and you gave me something to drink, I was a stranger and you welcomed me, I was naked and you gave me clothing, I was sick and you took care of me, I was in prison and you visited me. 'Then the righteous will answer him, 'Lord, when was it that we saw you hungry and gave you food, or thirsty and gave you something to drink? And when was it that we saw you a stranger and welcomed you, or naked and gave you clothing? And when was it that we saw you sick or in prison and visited you?' And the king will answer them, 'Truly I tell you, just as you did it to one of the least of these who are members of my family, you did it to me.'"

- This message is so simple, Lord. You will judge me on my love and service of others. You are there in the poor, the sick, the prisoners, the strangers. May I recognize your face.

Tuesday 27th February
Matthew 6:7–15

"When you are praying, do not heap up empty phrases as the Gentiles do; for they think that they will be heard because of their many words. Do not be like them, for your Father knows what you need before you ask him. "Pray then in this way: Our Father in heaven, hallowed be your name. Your kingdom come. Your will be done, on earth as it is in heaven. Give us this day our daily bread. And forgive us our debts, as we also have forgiven our debtors. And do not bring us to the time of trial, but rescue us from the evil one. For if you forgive others their trespasses, your heavenly Father will also forgive you; but if you do not forgive others, neither will your Father forgive your trespasses."

- Father, as I turn to you in prayer, you already know what I need. I do not change you by asking; I change myself.

- I may call God 'Abba'—my daddy. And I shall be forgiven as I forgive others. Can I be true to that relationship?

Wednesday 28th February
Psalm 50(51):1–3, 10–11, 16–17

Have mercy on me, O God, according to your steadfast love according to your abundant mercy blot out my transgressions. Wash me thoroughly from my iniquity, and cleanse me from my sin. For I know my transgressions, and my sin is ever before me. Create in me a clean heart, O God, and put a new and right spirit within me. Do not cast me away from your presence, and do not take your holy spirit from me. For you have no delight in sacrifice if I were to give a burnt offering, you would not be pleased. The sacrifice acceptable to God is a contrite spirit a humbled and contrite heart, O God, you will not spurn.

- "Wash me thoroughly . . . cleanse me. . . . Create in me a clean heart, O God." There is a good deal of scrubbing to do Lord. I need to keep a habitual sense of my weakness, to save me from arrogance.

* I have confidence that you will keep me close to your presence, and teach me to live in the Spirit. With a humbled heart.

Thursday 1st March   Matthew 7:7–11

Jesus said to the crowds, "Ask, and it will be given you; search, and you will find; knock, and the door will be opened for you. For everyone who asks receives, and everyone who searches finds, and for everyone who knocks, the door will be opened. Is there anyone among you who, if your child asks for bread, will give a stone? Or if the child asks for a fish, will give a snake? If you then, who are evil, know how to give good gifts to your children, how much more will your Father in heaven give good things to those who ask him!"

- "Ask . . . search . . . knock." Three aspects of prayer, each one giving us confidence of gaining a hearing. Jesus' teaching is demanding, but our Father is willing to give us the capacity if we but ask.

- With the confidence of the child, we can demand, "Give us this day our daily bread." Each day, we are invited to ask, to demand.

Friday 2nd March   Matthew 5:20–26

Jesus said to his disciples, "For I tell you, unless your righteousness exceeds that of the scribes and Pharisees, you will never enter the kingdom of heaven. You have heard that it was said to those of ancient times, 'You shall not murder'; and 'whoever murders shall be liable to judgment.' But I say to you that if you are angry with a brother or sister, you will be liable to judgment; and if you insult a brother or sister, you will be liable to the council; and if you say, 'You fool,' you will be liable to the hell of fire. So when you are offering your gift at the altar, if you remember that your brother or sister has something against you, leave your gift there before the altar and go; first be reconciled to your brother or sister, and then come and offer your gift. Come to terms quickly with your accuser while you are on the way to court with him, or your accuser may hand you over to the judge, and the judge to the guard, and you will be thrown into prison. Truly I tell you, you will never get out until you have paid the last penny."

- Jesus takes the law of Moses and makes it deeper, more interior. The root of the act of killing is in the angry hatred in the killer's heart. Tackle the evil at its source.

- It is not just a question of my anger or my guilt. Rather, if there is a rift, I must recognize it and work to heal it. Reconciliation with brother and sister is supremely important.

- Am I afraid this is too hard for me? Can I ask the Lord about it?

Saturday 3rd March   Matthew 5:43–48

Jesus said to the disciples, "You have heard that it was said, 'You shall love your neighbor and hate your enemy.' But I say to you, Love your enemies and pray for those who persecute you, so that you may be children of your Father in heaven; for he makes his sun rise on the evil and on the good, and sends rain on the righteous and on the unrighteous. For if you love those who love you, what reward do you have? Do not even the tax collectors do the same? And if you greet only your brothers and sisters, what more are you doing than others? Do not even the Gentiles do the same?

Be perfect, therefore, as your heavenly
Father is perfect."

- Lord, you teach us that the children of God
  are to go beyond the accepted standards.
  Our call is to act as the Creator acts towards
  all people, even towards our enemies.

- Is this is hopeless idealism or a wise strategy for overcoming the persecutor? Teach
  me to change aggression into a strategy for
  winning through the wisdom of love.

march 4–10

Something to think and pray about each day this week:

Transfiguration

When Peter saw Jesus transfigured on Tabor, he wanted to put up tents on the top of the mountain and settle down there. It was a peak experience, and he wanted it to go on for ever. But Jesus brought them down from the mountain, back to the level everyday routine.

I know, Lord, that we cannot live for ever on a charismatic high. I am lucky if from time to time you lift me out of myself. But for most of the time I have to be content with the routine of survival, living on faith, which is a mixture of light and darkness.

The Presence of God

For a few moments, I think of God's veiled
presence in things:
in the elements, giving them existence;
in plants, giving them life; in animals, giving
them sensation;
and finally, in me, giving me all this and
more, making me a temple, a dwelling-place
of the Spirit.

Freedom

God is not foreign to my freedom.
Instead the Spirit breathes life into my most
intimate desires, gently nudging me towards
all that is good.
I ask for the grace to let myself be enfolded
by the Spirit.

Consciousness

Knowing that God loves me unconditionally,
I can afford to be honest about how I am.

How has the last day been, and how do I feel now?

I share my feelings openly with the Lord.

The Word

I take my time to read the Word of God, slowly, a few times, allowing myself to dwell on anything that strikes me. (Please turn to your scripture on the following pages. Inspiration points are there should you need them. When you are ready, return here to continue.)

Conversation

How has God's Word moved me? Has it left me cold? Has it consoled me or moved me to act in a new way?

I imagine Jesus standing or sitting beside me, I turn and share my feelings with him.

Conclusion

Glory be to the Father, and to the Son, and to the Holy Spirit, As it was in the beginning, is now and ever shall be, World without end. Amen

Sunday 4th March
Second Sunday of Lent   Luke 9:28b–36

Now about eight days after these sayings Jesus took with him Peter and John and James, and went up on the mountain to pray. And while he was praying, the appearance of his face changed, and his clothes became dazzling white. Suddenly they saw two men, Moses and Elijah, talking to him. They appeared in glory and were speaking of his departure, which he was about to accomplish at Jerusalem. Now Peter and his companions were weighed down with sleep; but since they had stayed awake, they saw his glory and the two men who stood with him. Just as they were leaving him, Peter said to Jesus, "Master, it is good for us to be here; let us make three dwellings, one for you, one for Moses, and one for Elijah"—not knowing what he said. While he was saying this, a cloud came and overshadowed them; and they were terrified as they entered the cloud. Then from the cloud came a voice that said, "This is my Son, my Chosen; listen to him!" When the voice had spoken, Jesus was found alone. And they kept silent and in those days told no one any of the things they had seen.

- In this moment of "transfiguration" God the Father affirms Jesus for who he really is: "This is my Son, my Chosen." This must have been profoundly consoling. But, Jesus' being who he really was inevitably involved him going forward to do what he had to do.

- Can I allow the Father to affirm me for who I really am? Is there consolation for me?

- Does being who I really am hold any terrors for me?

Monday 5th March   Luke 6:36–38

Be merciful, just as your Father is merciful. "Do not judge, and you will not be judged; do not condemn, and you will not be condemned. Forgive, and you will be forgiven; give, and it will be given to you. A good measure, pressed down, shaken together, running over, will be put into your lap; for the measure you give will be the measure you get back."

- "The measure you give will be the measure you get back." God aims to be extravagantly generous with each of us; the limitations come from me.

- How do I place limits of God's generosity?

- Why do I do that? Am I fearful of what might happen to my life?

Tuesday 6th March   Matthew 23:8–12

Jesus said to the crowds and to his disciples, "You are not to be called rabbi, for you have one teacher, and you are all students. And call no one your father on earth, for you have one Father—the one in heaven. Nor are you to be called instructors, for you have one instructor, the Messiah. The greatest among you will be your servant. All who exalt themselves will be humbled, and all who humble themselves will be exalted."

• Jesus, you made yourself a baby, a child, a carpenter, my servant, a sufferer, and a victim of injustice. I know that when you teach me the Beatitudes, and tell me to love others, you speak from your human experience as well as being the Word of God.

• You know what you are asking. As St. Peter exclaimed: "Lord, to whom should we go?

You have the message of eternal life." May I always know you as my master.

Wednesday 7th March
Matthew 20:17–23

While Jesus was going up to Jerusalem, he took the twelve disciples aside by themselves, and said to them on the way, "See, we are going up to Jerusalem, and the Son of Man will be handed over to the chief priests and scribes, and they will condemn him to death; then they will hand him over to the Gentiles to be mocked and flogged and crucified; and on the third day he will be raised. Then the mother of the sons of Zebedee came to him with her sons, and kneeling before him, she asked a favour of him. And he said to her, "What do you want?" She said to him, "Declare that these two sons of mine will sit, one at your right hand and one at your left, in your kingdom." But

Jesus answered, "You do not know what you are asking. Are you able to drink the cup that I am about to drink?" They said to him, "We are able." He said to them, "You will indeed drink my cup, but to sit at my right hand and at my left, this is not mine to grant, but it is for those for whom it has been prepared by my Father."

- Is there a yearning within me for power and glory, for myself or close friend I look up to?

- Do I ever have a "magical" attitude to faith that would like to use God's power for my own ends?

Thursday 8th March   Jeremiah 17:5–8

Thus says the Lord: Cursed are those who trust in mere mortals and make mere flesh their strength, whose hearts turn away from the Lord. They shall be like a shrub in the desert, and shall not see when relief comes. They shall live in the parched places of the wilderness, in an uninhabited salt land. Blessed are those who trust in the Lord, whose trust is the Lord. They shall be like a tree planted by water, sending out its roots by the stream. It shall not fear when heat comes, and its leaves shall stay green; in the year of drought it is not anxious, and it does not cease to bear fruit.

- The one who trusts in the Lord is like a tree planted by water, "sending out its roots by the stream." I know, Lord, what dryness, desolation and sterility feel like.

- Let me pray with you.

Friday 9th March
Matthew 21:33–43, 45–46

Jesus said: "Listen to another parable. There was a landowner who planted a vineyard, put a fence around it, dug a wine press in it, and built a watchtower. Then he leased it to tenants and went to another country. When the harvest time had come, he sent his slaves to the tenants to collect his produce. But the tenants seized his slaves and beat one, killed another, and stoned another. Again he sent other slaves, more than the first; and they treated them in the same way. Finally he sent his son to them, saying, 'They will respect my son.' But when the tenants saw the son, they said to themselves, 'This is the heir; come, let us kill him and get his inheritance.' So they seized him, threw him out of the vineyard, and killed him. Now when the owner of the vineyard comes, what will he do to those tenants?" They said to him, "He will put those wretches to a miserable death, and lease the vineyard to other tenants who will give him the produce at the harvest time." Jesus said to them, "Have you never read in the scriptures: 'The stone that the builders rejected has become the cornerstone; this was the Lord's doing, and it is amazing in our eyes'?

Therefore I tell you, the kingdom of God will be taken away from you and given to a people that produces the fruits of the kingdom. When the chief priests and the Pharisees heard his parables, they realized that he was speaking about them. They wanted to arrest him, but they feared the crowds, because they regarded him as a prophet."

- Lord, this parable is about the Jews, but also about me. I am the tenant of your vineyard. For me you have planted and protected a crop, and from me you expect some harvest.

- The fruit of my labors is for you, not for me. I may feel annoyed when you ask, but you are right to expect something of me.

Saturday 10th March
Micah 7:14–15, 18–20

Shepherd your people with your staff, the flock that belongs to you, which lives alone in a forest in the midst of a garden land; let them feed in Bashan and Gilead as in the days of old. As in the days when you came out of the land of Egypt, show us marvelous things. Who is a God like you, pardoning iniquity and passing over the transgression of the remnant of your possession? He does not retain his anger forever, because he delights in showing clemency. He will again have compassion upon us; he will tread our iniquities under foot. You will cast all our sins into the depths of the sea. You will show faithfulness to Jacob and unswerving loyalty to Abraham, as you have sworn to our ancestors from the days of old.

- "He does not retain his anger for ever, because he delights in steadfast love." The parable of the Prodigal Son shows me how steadfast that love is.

- Can I accept that you pardon me Lord, do not retain anger against me, and that you even take delight in me? Let me talk with you about this.

Something to think and pray about each day this week:

Spreading the Word

If there is a hierarchy in heaven based on the churches named after you, Patrick must be at the top. He is our antidote to racism—a Welsh boy educated in France and missioned by Italians, who became the loved apostle of Ireland, and the toast of Irish people everywhere on 17th March. He is our antidote to conservatism—a slave who ran away from his owners and returned to Ireland to face down kings and chieftains. He was a visionary who followed his dreams, and loved the high mountains like Slemish and Croagh

Patrick. Above all he was a religious man who turned to God during his leisured hours as a swineherd.

All through his Confessions you sense his overflowing gratitude for the privilege of knowing Almighty God and Jesus Christ his son as he wrote: "In the light of our faith in the Trinity, regardless of danger, I must make known the gift of God and ever-lasting consolation, without fear and frankly. I must spread everywhere the name of God so that after my decease I may leave a bequest to those whom I have baptized in the Lord; so many thousands of people."

The Presence of God

I pause for a moment and think of the love and the grace that God showers on me, creating me in his image and likeness, making me his temple.

Freedom

Everything has the potential to draw forth from me a fuller love and life.
Yet my desires are often fixed, caught, on illusions of fulfillment.
I ask that God, through my freedom, may orchestrate my desires in a vibrant loving melody rich in harmony.

Consciousness

In the presence of my loving Creator,
I look honestly at my feelings over the last day, the highs, the lows and the level ground.
Can I see where the Lord has been present?

The Word

God speaks to each one of us individually. I need to listen to what he is saying to me. (Please turn to your scripture on the following pages. Inspiration points are there should you need them. When you are ready, return here to continue.)

Conversation

What feelings are rising in me
as I pray and reflect on God's Word?
I imagine Jesus himself sitting or standing beside me,
and open my heart to him.

Conclusion

Glory be to the Father, and to the Son, and to the Holy Spirit,
As it was in the beginning, is now and ever shall be,
World without end. Amen

Sunday 11th March
Third Sunday of Lent   Luke 13:1–9

At that very time there were some present who told him about the Galileans whose blood Pilate had mingled with their sacrifices. He asked them, "Do you think that because these Galileans suffered in this way they were worse sinners than all other Galileans? No, I tell you; but unless you repent, you will all perish as they did. Or those eighteen who were killed when the tower of Siloam fell on them—do you think that they were worse offenders than all the others living in Jerusalem? No, I tell you; but unless you repent, you will all perish just as they did." Then he told this parable: "A man had a fig tree planted in his vineyard; and he came looking for fruit on it and found none. So he said to the gardener, 'See here! For three years I have come looking for fruit on this fig tree, and still I find none. Cut it down! Why should it be wasting the soil?' He replied, 'Sir, let it alone for one more year, until I dig around it and put manure on it. If it bears fruit next year, well and good; but if not, you can cut it down.'"

- Do I hear different voices of judgment in the passage? What do they spark in me?

- What about the gardener? What does he say?

- Is there a tendency towards harsh judgment in me—towards others or towards myself?

- Can I hear the voice of the gardener speaking within me?

Monday 12th March   Luke 4:24–30

And he said, "Truly I tell you, no prophet is accepted in the prophet's hometown. But the truth is, there were many widows in Israel in the time of Elijah, when the heaven was shut up three years and six months, and there was a severe famine over all the land;

yet Elijah was sent to none of them except to a widow at Zarephath in Sidon. There were also many lepers in Israel in the time of the prophet Elisha, and none of them was cleansed except Naaman the Syrian." When they heard this, all in the synagogue were filled with rage. They got up, drove him out of the town, and led him to the brow of the hill on which their town was built, so that they might hurl him off the cliff. But he passed through the midst of them and went on his way.

- Jesus' story reminds us of the self-important Naaman who felt he had been slighted when Elisha did not attend upon the great man personally, but sent a messenger with a simple instruction.

- I am the same, Lord. Do I become angry or stand back when my expectations are not met? Even when I need you greatly? I want not just a cure, but to be the centre of attention.

Tuesday 13th March Matthew 18:21–35

Then Peter came and said to him, "Lord, if another member of the church sins against me, how often should I forgive? As many as seven times?" Jesus said to him, "Not seven times, but, I tell you, seventy-seven times. "For this reason the kingdom of heaven may be compared to a king who wished to settle accounts with his slaves. When he began the reckoning, one who owed him ten thousand talents was brought to him; and, as he could not pay, his lord ordered him to be sold, together with his wife and children and all his possessions, and payment to be made. So the slave fell on his knees before him, saying, 'Have patience with me, and I will pay you everything.' And out of pity for him, the lord of that slave released him and forgave him the debt. But that same slave, as he went out, came upon one of his fellow slaves who owed him a hundred denarii; and seizing him by the throat, he said, 'Pay what you owe.' Then his fellow slave fell down and pleaded with him, 'Have patience with me, and I will pay you.' But he refused; then he went and threw him into prison until he would pay the debt. When his fellow slaves saw what had happened, they were greatly distressed, and they went and reported to their lord all that had taken place. Then his lord summoned him and said to him, 'You wicked slave! I forgave you all that debt because you pleaded with me. Should you not have had mercy on your fellow slave, as I had mercy on you?' And in anger his lord handed him over to be tortured until he would pay his entire debt. So my heavenly Father will also do to every one of you, if you do not forgive your brother or sister from your heart."

- The servant is forgiven a huge debt he could not hope to repay—justice is completely overwhelmed by mercy. In that light, his refusal to his own debtor is even more monstrous and brutal.

- Lord, do I choose harsh justice for others when mercy could be extended? Will I find hypocrisy in my words, my attitudes, my actions? Can I look hard at this?

Wednesday 14th March
Matthew 5:17–19

Do not think that I have come to abolish the law or the prophets; I have come not to abolish but to fulfill. For truly I tell you, until heaven and earth pass away, not one letter, not one stroke of a letter, will pass from the law until all is accomplished. Therefore, whoever breaks one of the least of these commandments, and teaches others to do the same, will be called least in the kingdom of heaven; but whoever does them and teaches them will be called great in the kingdom of heaven.

- Jesus did not reject the Old Testament of the Jews, but brought it back to its essentials: love God and love your neighbor. Our life should be whole—people should be able to read our principles from our behavior.

- It is harder to live one sermon than to preach a dozen.

Thursday 15th March
Jeremiah 7:23–28

But this command I gave them, "Obey my voice, and I will be your God, and you shall be my people; and walk only in the way that I command you, so that it may be well with you." Yet they did not obey or incline their ear, but, in the stubbornness of their evil will, they walked in their own counsels, and looked backward rather than forward. From the day that your ancestors came out of the land of Egypt until this day, I have persistently sent all my servants the prophets to them, day after day; yet they did not listen to me, or pay attention, but they stiffened their necks. They did worse than their ancestors did. So you shall speak all these words to them, but they will not listen to you. You shall call to them, but they will not answer you. You shall say to them: This is the nation that did not obey the voice of the Lord their God, and did not accept discipline; truth has perished; it is cut off from their lips.

- "Obey my voice, and I will be your God, and you shall be my people." In the dialogue between God and humanity, there is the give-and-take of constant self-revelation and response; as with any relationship.

• Yet I often find it so hard, Lord, to respond positively. I look to my own ways, while you remain open and loving in the face of my persistent stubbornness. Open my heart to your love.

Friday 16th March   Mark 12:28–34

One of the scribes came near and heard them disputing with one another, and seeing that he answered them well, he asked him, "Which commandment is the first of all?" Jesus answered, "The first is, 'Hear, O Israel: the Lord our God, the Lord is one; you shall love the Lord your God with all your heart, and with all your soul, and with all your mind, and with all your strength.' The second is this, 'You shall love your neighbor as yourself.' There is no other commandment greater than these." Then the scribe said to him, "You are right, Teacher; you have truly said that 'he is one, and besides him there is no other'; and 'to love him with all the heart, and with all the understanding, and with all the strength,' and 'to love one's neighbor as oneself,'—this is much more important than all whole burnt offerings and sacrifices." When Jesus saw that he answered wisely, he said to him, "You are not far from the kingdom of God." After that no one dared to ask him any question.

- The scribe is not hostile but a sincere person, seeking the truth. He is deeply impressed with the answer Jesus gives him; Jesus is equally impressed with the scribe's understanding.

- How do I measure up here? Are my religious observances more important than my relationships with God and neighbor?

Am I reconciled with others or in dispute?
How far am I from the kingdom of God?

Saturday 17th March
St. Patrick   Isaiah 52:7–10

How beautiful upon the mountains are the feet of the messenger who announces peace, who brings good news, who announces salvation, who says to Zion, "Your God reigns." Listen! Your sentinels lift up their voices, together they sing for joy; for in plain sight they see the return of the Lord to Zion. Break forth together into singing, you ruins of Jerusalem; for the Lord has comforted his people, he has redeemed Jerusalem. The Lord has bared his holy arm before the eyes of all the nations; and all the ends of the earth shall see the salvation of our God.

- How important are the heroes in my life, the men and women to whom I look up, now or when I was younger?

- Do I think of Jesus as my hero? Do I have a particular hero among the people who brought the good news to me or to my ancestors? Can I ask for their support?

Something to think and pray about each day this week:

Faithful insecurity
Imagine walking unassisted in a darkened room. I move my hands around in front of my body, lest I bump into a wall, a piece of furniture and come to grief.

This is not dissimilar from what God calls us to on the journey of faith. It is not easy for us, as we want to have our pathways well signposted. We want to know where, how, why, and when we are moving. Faith, though, is the security to be insecure. Our trust is in God, and not in our own charm, intelligence or insight, our status or power.

The Presence of God

I reflect for a moment on God's presence
around me and in me.
Creator of the universe, the sun and the
moon, the earth,
every molecule, every atom, everything
that is:
God is in every beat of my heart. God is
with me, now.

Freedom

A thick and shapeless tree trunk would
never believe that it could become a statue,
admired as a miracle of sculpture,
and would never submit itself to the chisel
of the sculptor,
who sees by her genius what she can make
of it. (St. Ignatius)
I ask for the grace to let myself be shaped
by my loving Creator.

Consciousness

Knowing that God loves me unconditionally, I look honestly over the last day, its events and my feelings.

Do I have something to be grateful for? Then I give thanks.

Is there something I am sorry for? Then I ask forgiveness.

The Word

I read the Word of God slowly, a few times over, and I listen to what God is saying to me. (Please turn to your scripture on the following pages. Inspiration points are there should you need them. When you are ready, return here to continue.)

Conversation

What is stirring in me as I pray?

Am I consoled, troubled, left cold?

I imagine Jesus himself standing or sitting at my side,

and share my feelings with him.

Conclusion

Glory be to the Father, and to the Son, and to the Holy Spirit,
As it was in the beginning, is now and ever shall be,
World without end. Amen

Sunday 18th March
Fourth Sunday of Lent   Luke 15:12–24

Then Jesus said, "There was a man who had two sons. The younger of them said to his father, 'Father, give me the share of the property that will belong to me.' So he divided his property between them. A few days later the younger son gathered all he had and traveled to a distant country, and there he squandered his property in dissolute living. When he had spent everything, a severe famine took place throughout that country, and he began to be in need. So he went and hired himself out to one of the citizens of that country, who sent him to his fields to feed the pigs. He would gladly have filled himself with the pods that the pigs were eating; and no one gave him anything. But when he came to himself he said, 'How many of my father's hired hands have bread enough and to spare, but here I am dying of hunger! I will get up and go to my father, and I will say to him, "Father, I have sinned against heaven and before you; I am no longer worthy to be called your son; treat me like one of your hired hands."' So he set off and went to his father. But while he was still far off, his father saw him and was filled with compassion; he ran and put his arms around him and kissed him. Then the son said to him, 'Father, I have sinned against heaven and before you; I am no longer worthy to be called your son.' But the father said to his slaves, 'Quickly, bring out a robe—the best one—and put it on him; put a ring on his finger and sandals on his feet. And get the fatted calf and kill it, and let us eat and celebrate; for this son of mine was dead and is alive again; he was lost and is found!' And they began to celebrate."

- When I do a quick scan of this story, where does my gaze lie? Is it on the abandonment, the dream gone sour, the degradation and squalor? Or, do I go straight to the picture of the father scanning the horizon, the compassion, the reconciliation and the forgiveness?

- My spontaneous inclination might tell me something about what I need to learn from this scripture.

- Where am I in my journey? Am I walking out the door? Am I in a foreign land? Or, am I on the way home?

Monday 19th March
St. Joseph   Matthew 1:18–25

Now the birth of Jesus the Messiah took place in this way. When his mother Mary had been engaged to Joseph, but before they lived together, she was found to be with child from the Holy Spirit. Her husband Joseph, being a righteous man and unwilling to expose her to public disgrace, planned to dismiss her quietly. But just when he had resolved to do this, an angel of the Lord appeared to him in a dream and said, "Joseph, son of David, do not be afraid to take Mary as your wife, for the child conceived in her is from the Holy Spirit. She will bear a son, and you are to name him Jesus, for he will save his people from their sins." All this took place to fulfill what had been spoken by the Lord through the prophet: "Look, the virgin shall conceive and bear a son, and they shall name him Emmanuel," which means, "God is with us." When Joseph awoke from sleep, he did as the angel of the Lord commanded him; he took her as his wife, but had no marital relations with her until she had borne a son; and he named him Jesus.

- How do we think about St. Joseph? Yes, he receives the news of the annunciation, and he is there with Mary during her pregnancy and the birth of Jesus. But he is also the man working to support his family for many years, providing guidance, education and example to the young Jesus.

- Can I imagine the everyday life of Joseph, with the young Jesus trailing behind him, copying his actions, listening carefully to what he said? What did Joseph observe in this growing boy? What glimpses of the future did he see?

Tuesday 20th March   John 5:1–8

After this there was a festival of the Jews, and Jesus went up to Jerusalem. Now in Jerusalem by the Sheep Gate there is a pool, called in Hebrew Beth-zatha, which has five porticoes. In these lay many invalids—blind, lame, and paralyzed. One man was there who had been ill for thirty-eight years. When Jesus saw him lying there and knew that he had been there a long time, he said to him, "Do you want to be made well?" The sick man answered him, "Sir, I have no one to put me into the pool when the water is stirred up; and while I am making my way, someone else steps down ahead of me." Jesus said to him, "Stand up, take your mat and walk."

- "Do you want to be made well?" It looks obvious to a healthy person but the question makes sense, because a cure would change his life completely.

- Lord, I do want to be healed, to change my life and take on all that you may ask of me.

Wednesday 21st March
Isaiah 49:13–15

For the Lord has comforted his people, and will have compassion on his suffering ones. But Zion said, "The Lord has forsaken me, my Lord has forgotten me. "Can a woman forget her nursing child, or show no compassion for the child of her womb? Even these may forget, yet I will not forget you."

- Here is a reminder of the motherhood of God: "Can a woman forget her nursing child, or show no compassion for the child of her womb? Even these may forget, yet I will not forget you."

- My God, you tell me that for you I am unique, and that I have a place in your mind which nobody else can fill. You regard me with the delight and tenderness of a mother with her baby.

Thursday 22nd March   John 5:44–47

Jesus said to the Jews, "How can you believe when you accept glory from one another and do not seek the glory that comes from the one who alone is God? Do not think that I will accuse you before the Father; your accuser is Moses, on whom you have set your hope. If you believed

Moses, you would believe me, for he wrote about me. But if you do not believe what he wrote, how will you believe what I say?"

- This reading reflects the nub of the struggle between God and his chosen people, the Jews. It says something to us too: our desire to seek human glory and admiration from others while refusing to see and accept the signs of God's presence.

- Lord, draw me out from my closed-in world, from my own cosy groups where I am sure of my world, and frightened of being opened up to the new, in your name.

Friday 23rd March Wisdom 2:1, 12–15

For the godless reasoned unsoundly, saying to themselves, "Short and sorrowful is our life, and there is no remedy when a life comes to its end, and no one has been known to return from Hades. Let us lie in wait for the righteous man, because he is inconvenient to us and opposes our actions; he reproaches us for sins against the law, and accuses us of sins against our training. He professes to have knowledge of God, and calls himself a child of the Lord. He became to us a reproof of our thoughts; the very sight of him is a burden to us, because his manner of life is unlike that of others, and his ways are strange."

- "He became to us a reproof of our thoughts; the very sight of him is a burden to us." You touch me where it hurts, Lord, when you describe the jealousy we often feel for somebody whose life is different.

- Lord, make my heart more generous, so that I rejoice in the goodness of others.

Saturday 24th March
Annunciation of the Lord
Luke 1:26–32, 34–35, 38a

In the sixth month the angel Gabriel was sent by God to a town in Galilee called Nazareth, to a virgin whose name was Mary. And he came to her and said, "Greetings, favored one! The Lord is with you." But she was much perplexed by his words and pondered what sort of greeting this might be. The angel said to her, "Do not be afraid, Mary, for you have found favor with God. And now, you will conceive in your womb and bear a son, and you will name him Jesus. He will be great, and will be called the Son of the Most High, and the Lord God will give to him the throne of his ancestor David." Mary said to the angel, "How can this be, since I am a virgin?" The angel said to her, "The Holy Spirit will come upon you, and the power of the Most High will overshadow you; therefore the child to be born will be holy; he will be called Son of God." Then Mary said, "Here am I, the servant of the Lord; let it be with me according to your word."

- Can I take the time to think about these events, to imagine what Mary felt as she was given this awesome news.

- Mary has questions and voices them, but she says "Yes" to God's will for her. Can I learn from her example?

march 25–31

Something to think and pray about each day this week:

The place of prayer

Prayer is a spiritual place, a psychological place, a place where we go to get out of ourselves, a place created by and inhabited by our God. Whatever disciplines can help us to get to where God's reality can get at us, are those we should embrace.

Prayer isn't bending God's power in order to get things we want, or talking God into seeing things our way. It is whatever calls us to detach from our own self, from our own compulsions and addictions, from our own ego, from our own cozy space. We are all too trapped in our own places by virtue of the egocentricity of the human person. In prayer the Spirit entices us outside our narrow comfort zone.

No wonder we avoid prayer: We have to change places, to move to a sacred space.

The Presence of God

In the silence of my innermost being,
in the fragments of my yearned-for wholeness,
can I hear the whispers of God's presence?
Can I remember when I felt God's nearness?
When we walked together and I let myself
be embraced by God's love.

Freedom

There are very few people who realize what
God would make of them if they abandoned themselves into his hands, and let
themselves be formed by his grace. (St.
Ignatius) I ask for the grace to trust myself
totally to God's love.

Consciousness

How do I find myself today?
Where am I with God? With others?
Do I have something to be grateful for?
Then I give thanks.
Is there something I am sorry for? Then I
ask forgiveness.

The Word

I take my time to read the Word of God, slowly, a few times, allowing myself to dwell on anything that strikes me. (Please turn to your scripture on the following pages. Inspiration points are there should you need them. When you are ready, return here to continue.)

Conversation

Do I notice myself reacting as I pray with the Word of God?
Do I feel challenged, comforted, angry?
Imagining Jesus sitting or standing by me, I speak out my feelings, as one trusted friend to another.

Conclusion

Glory be to the Father, and to the Son, and to the Holy Spirit,
As it was in the beginning, is now and ever shall be,
World without end. Amen

Sunday 25th March
Fifth Sunday of Lent   John 8:2–11

Early in the morning Jesus came again to the temple. All the people came to him and he sat down and began to teach them. The scribes and the Pharisees brought a woman who had been caught in adultery; and making her stand before all of them, they said to him, "Teacher, this woman was caught in the very act of committing adultery. Now in the law Moses commanded us to stone such women. Now what do you say?" They said this to test him, so that they might have some charge to bring against him. Jesus bent down and wrote with his finger on the ground. When they kept on questioning him, he straightened up and said to them, "Let anyone among you who is without sin be the first to throw a stone at her." And once again he bent down and wrote on the ground. When they heard it, they went away, one by one, beginning with the elders; and Jesus was left alone with the woman standing before him. Jesus straightened up and said to her, "Woman, where are they? Has no one condemned you?" She said, "No one, sir." And Jesus said, "Neither do I condemn you. Go your way, and from now on do not sin again."

- I try to imagine this scene in the temple area with people coming and going. Suddenly there is a commotion. An angry crowd comes to Jesus, parading a solitary woman in front of him.

- What is happening? Do I identify with any of the characters in the scene? Which one?

- How does Jesus react? How does his reaction touch me?

Monday 26th March
Daniel 13:55–56, 60–62

Daniel said, "Indeed! Your lie recoils on you own head: the angel of God has already received from him your sentence and will cut you in half." He dismissed the man, ordered the other to be brought and said to him, "Son of Canaan, not of Huday, beauty has seduced you, lust has led your heart astray!" Then the whole assembly shouted, blessing God, the Savior of those who trust in him. And they turned on the two elders whom Daniel had convicted of false evidence out of their own mouths. As the Law of Moses prescribes, they were given the same punishment as they had schemed to inflict on their neighbor. They were put to death. And thus, that day, an innocent life was saved.

- "Beauty has seduced you, lust has led your heart astray." Plenty of others—more men than women—have followed those old men in being led by lust into personal disaster.

• Incitement to lust is all around us. We can ask the Lord to guide us away from these temptations, and keep us centered on God.

Tuesday 27th March   Numbers 21:4–9

From Mount Hor they set out by the way to the Red Sea, to go around the land of Edom; but the people became impatient on the way. The people spoke against God and against Moses, "Why have you brought us up out of Egypt to die in the wilderness? For there is no food and no water, and we detest this miserable food." Then the Lord sent poisonous serpents among the people, and they bit the people, so that many Israelites died. The people came to Moses and said, "We have sinned by speaking against the Lord and against you; pray to the Lord to take away the serpents from us." So Moses prayed for the people. And the Lord said to Moses, "Make a poisonous serpent, and set it on a pole; and everyone who is bitten shall look at it and live." So Moses made a serpent of bronze, and put it upon a pole; and whenever a serpent bit someone, that person would look at the serpent of bronze and live.

- The Book of Numbers tells a story of people complaining, being punished, turning to God, and finding relief.

- Lord, you have often taught me like a strict parent. You lead me to more abundant life through pruning and pain.

Wednesday 28th March   John 8:31–32

Then Jesus said to the Jews who had believed in him, "If you continue in my word, you are truly my disciples; and you will know the truth, and the truth will make you free."

- "The truth will make you free." We are often confused by this word "free." It has a cost; we have to pay a price. Throughout history, men and women have stood up against abusive power, without fear for their lives, to win freedom.

- Have I experienced the freedom that comes from truth? Or have I felt trapped by my fear of the truth?

- Can I speak to the Lord about this?

Thursday 29th March   Genesis 17:3–8

Then Abram fell on his face; and God said to him, "As for me, this is my covenant with you: You shall be the ancestor of a multitude of nations. No longer shall your name be Abram, but your name shall be Abraham; for I have made you the ancestor of a multitude of nations. I will make you exceedingly fruitful; and I will make nations of you, and kings shall come from you. I will establish my covenant between me and you, and your offspring after you throughout their generations, for an everlasting covenant, to be God to you and to your offspring after you. And I will give to you, and to your offspring after you, the land where you are now an alien, all the land of Canaan, for a perpetual holding; and I will be their God."

- God made a "covenant" with Abram. It was a new start for the man and his descendants, and with it his new name—Abraham.

- How does God's covenant with Abraham embrace me?

Friday 30th March   John 10:31–42

The Jews took up stones again to stone him. Jesus replied, "I have shown you many good works from the Father. For which of these are you going to stone me?" The Jews answered, "It is not for a good work that we are going to stone you, but for blasphemy, because you, though only a human being, are making yourself God." Jesus answered, "Is it not written in your law, 'I said, you are gods'? If those to whom the word of God came were called 'gods'— and the scripture cannot be annulled—can you say that the one whom the Father has sanctified and sent into the world is blaspheming because I said, 'I am God's Son'? If I am not doing the works of my Father, then do not believe me. But if I do them, even though you do not believe me, believe the works, so that you may know and understand that the Father is in me and I am in the Father." Then they tried to arrest him again, but he escaped from their hands. He went away again across the Jordan to the place where John had been baptizing earlier, and he remained there. Many came to him, and they were saying, "John performed no sign, but everything that John said about this man was true." And many believed in him there.

- "If I am not doing the works of my Father, then do not believe me." Love is shown not so much in words as in deeds. We are bombarded with words, by advertisers, politicians, media and every sort of preacher.

- To each of these, as to myself, I say: If your works do not square with your words, then I will not believe you.

- How do I measure up?

Saturday 31st March   Ezekiel 37:26–28

I will make a covenant of peace with them; it shall be an everlasting covenant with them; and I will bless them and multiply them, and will set my sanctuary among them forevermore. My dwelling place shall be with them; and I will be their God, and they shall be my people. Then the nations shall know that I the Lord sanctify Israel, when my sanctuary is among them forevermore.

- "It shall be an everlasting covenant with them." Ezekiel records that God's loving plan is renewed with a people, even though they have abandoned and betrayed him.

- There is a plan for me, no matter what has happened.

- What does this say to me?

Something to think and pray about each day this week:

Prayer of the Cross
This is Holy Week. Through our life we struggle against suffering and evil. We strive for happiness by our nature. But there are times when we cannot beat evil, only endure it, as when we face a wasting sickness, or betrayal by a loved one. At those times our only recourse is to Jesus in his passion. Our prayer then is desolate, the fruit of faith, that is to say, of darkness. In that obscure faith the understanding must be left behind, in order to go to God by love. It is the prayer of Jesus in

Gethsemane, a prayer so painful that he sweated blood. We do not look for this sort of cross, but when it comes, prayer centered on the crucifix may be the only thing that can save us from drink or dementia.

The Presence of God

God is with me, but more,
God is within me, giving me existence.
Let me dwell for a moment on God's life-giving presence in my body, my mind, my heart and in the whole of my life.

Freedom

I ask for the grace to believe in what I could be and do if I only allowed God, my loving Creator, to continue to create me, guide me and shape me.

Consciousness

I exist in a web of relationships—links to nature, people, God.
I trace out these links, giving thanks for the life that flows through them.
Some links are twisted or broken: I may feel regret, anger, disappointment.
I pray for the gift of acceptance and forgiveness.

The Word

I read the Word of God slowly, a few times over, and I listen to what God is saying to me. (Please turn to your scripture on the following pages. Inspiration points are there should you need them. When you are ready, return here to continue.)

Conversation

How has God's Word moved me? Has it left me cold?
Has it consoled me or moved me to act in a new way?
I imagine Jesus standing or sitting beside me, I turn and share my feelings with him.

Conclusion

Glory be to the Father, and to the Son, and to the Holy Spirit,
As it was in the beginning, is now and ever shall be,
World without end. Amen

Sunday 1st April
Palm Sunday of the Lord's Passion
Philippians 2:6–11

Let the same mind be in you that was in Christ Jesus, who, though he was in the form of God, did not regard equality with God as something to be exploited, but emptied himself, taking the form of a slave, being born in human likeness. And being found in human form, he humbled himself and became obedient to the point of death—even death on a cross. Therefore God also highly exalted him and gave him the name that is above every name, so that at the name of Jesus every knee should bend, in heaven and on earth and under the earth, and every tongue should confess that Jesus Christ is Lord, to the glory of God the Father.

• As Holy Week begins, I fix my eyes on Jesus. Simply mulling over the words of this beautiful early Christian hymn can help me appreciate the mystery of it.

Monday 2nd April   Isaiah 42:1–4

Here is my servant, whom I uphold, my chosen, in whom my soul delights; I have put my spirit upon him; he will bring forth justice to the nations. He will not cry or lift up his voice, or make it heard in the street; a bruised reed he will not break, and a dimly burning wick he will not quench; he will faithfully bring forth justice. He will not grow faint or be crushed until he has established justice in the earth; and the coastlands wait for his teaching.

- "He will not grow faint or be crushed until he has established justice in the earth; and the coastlands wait for his teaching."

- That is our mission too, Lord: not to succumb to pressure but by firm persistence, to establish justice on the earth, and to go forth with his teaching on our lips.

Tuesday 3rd April
John 13:21–27, 31–33, 36–38

After saying this Jesus was troubled in spirit, and declared, "Very truly, I tell you, one of you will betray me." The disciples looked at one another, uncertain of whom he was speaking. One of his disciples—the one whom Jesus loved—was reclining next to him; Simon Peter therefore motioned to him to ask Jesus of whom he was speaking. So while reclining next to Jesus, he asked him, "Lord, who is it?" Jesus answered, "It is the one to whom I give this piece of bread when I have dipped it in the dish." So when he had dipped the piece of bread, he gave it to Judas son of Simon Iscariot. After he received the piece of bread, Satan entered into him. Jesus said to him, "Do quickly what you are going to do." . . . When Judas had gone out, Jesus said, "Now the Son of Man has been glorified, and God has been glorified in him. If God has been glorified in him, God will also glorify him in himself and will glorify him at once. Little children, I am with you only a little longer. You will look for me; and as I said to the Jews so now I say to you, 'Where I am going, you cannot come.' Simon Peter said to him, "Lord, where are you going?" Jesus answered, "Where I am going, you cannot follow me now; but you will follow afterward." Peter said to him, "Lord, why can I not follow you now? I will lay down my life for you." Jesus answered, "Will you lay down your life for me? Very truly, I tell you, before the cock crows, you will have denied me three times."

- Two treacheries: Judas went out to grab his money, betray Jesus, and kill himself in despair. Peter despite his protests would deny his Lord; he faced his own appalling guilt, wept bitterly, and his failure was not the end of his mission, but the beginning.

- Success is what I do with my failures. Teach me to trust in your love, Lord, and to learn from my mistakes and treacheries.

Wednesday 4th April
Matthew 26:14–16

Then one of the twelve, who was called Judas Iscariot, went to the chief priests and said, "What will you give me if I betray him to you?" They paid him thirty pieces of silver. And from that moment he began to look for an opportunity to betray him.

- Judas' greatest mistake was not that he betrayed Jesus, but that he had no confidence in the Lord's mercy and in his own power to recover from that betrayal, as Peter did. Am I confident?

Thursday 5th April
Holy Thursday   John 13:12–16

After Jesus had washed their feet, had put on his robe, and had returned to the table, he said to them, "Do you know what I have done to you? You call me Teacher and Lord—and you are right, for that is what I am. So if I, your Lord and Teacher, have washed your feet, you also ought to wash one another's feet. For I have set you an example, that you also should do as I have done to you. Very truly, I tell you, servants are not greater than their master, nor are messengers greater than the one who sent them."

- John's gospel describes the Last Supper by describing how Jesus washed his friends' feet, an act of service integral to discipleship.

- On his knees like a servant, Jesus turned human status upside down. Do I understand what he had done?

Friday 6th April
Good Friday   Isaiah 53:1–5

Who has believed what we have heard? And to whom has the arm of the Lord been revealed? For he grew up before him like a young plant, and like a root out of dry ground; he had no form or majesty that we should look at him, nothing in his appearance that we should desire him. He was despised and rejected by others; a man of suffering and acquainted with infirmity; and as one from whom others hide their faces he was despised, and we held him of no account. Surely he has borne our infirmities and carried our diseases; yet we accounted him stricken, struck down by God, and afflicted. But he was wounded for our transgressions, crushed for our iniquities; upon him was the punishment that made us whole, and by his bruises we are healed.

- Now we are at the heart of Jesus' mission: to suffer appallingly and to die without faltering in his love for us. This is where the Gospel begins and ends.

- Love demands that we trust in a goodness and a life beyond our own. Lord, it is hard to contemplate. I shy away from the pain and injustice of this Cross. Your love draws me back.

Saturday 7th April
Holy Saturday   Romans 6:3–9

Do you not know that all of us who have been baptized into Christ Jesus were baptized into his death? Therefore we have been buried with him by baptism into death, so that, just as Christ was raised from the dead by the glory of the Father, so we too might walk in newness of life. For if we have been united with him in a death like his, we will certainly be united with him in a resurrection like his. We know that our old self was crucified with him so that the body of sin might be destroyed, and we might no longer be enslaved to sin. For whoever has died is freed from sin. But if we have died with Christ, we believe that we will also live with him. We know that Christ, being raised from the dead, will never die again; death no longer has dominion over him.

- Tonight we re-affirm our ancient faith: Christ has robbed death of its ultimate sting, and has invigorated this sweet, precious, precarious, once-only life that is slipping away from us with every hour and day and year.

- To be Christian means to be an optimist because we know that Jesus' death was not in vain; his leap of faith was not in vain; his trust in his Father was not in vain. God raised him up.

Something to think and pray about each day this week:

Risen into life

On the first Easter morning, the apostles and the holy women did not see a ghost of Jesus. They saw him in the flesh, but in a different flesh, as the oak tree is different from the acorn that was its origin. We touch on the mystery of a body, not just Jesus' body but our own, which will express us at our best, will not blunt our spirit with weariness and rebellion, but express it with ease and joy. This is a mystery beyond our imagination, but it is the centre of our faith. As we grow older, nothing in our faith makes more sense than the Passion and the Resurrection, the certainty that our body, like Jesus', must suffer and die, and the certainty that we, in our bodies, have a life beyond death.

The Presence of God

To be present is to arrive as one is and open up to the other.

At this instant, as I arrive here, God is present waiting for me.

God always arrives before me, desiring to connect with me even more than my most intimate friend.

I take a moment and greet my loving God.

Freedom

"In these days, God taught me as a schoolteacher teaches a pupil" (St. Ignatius).

I remind myself that there are things God has to teach me yet, and ask for the grace to hear them and let them change me.

Consciousness

How am I really feeling? Light-hearted? Heavy-hearted?

I may be very much at peace, happy to be here. Equally, I may be frustrated, worried or angry.

I acknowledge how I really am. It is the real me that the Lord loves.

The Word
I take my time to read the Word of God, slowly, a few times, allowing myself to dwell on anything that strikes me. (Please turn to your scripture on the following pages. Inspiration points are there should you need them. When you are ready, return here to continue.)

Conversation
What feelings are rising in me
as I pray and reflect on God's Word?
I imagine Jesus himself sitting or standing beside me, and open my heart to him.

Conclusion
Glory be to the Father, and to the Son, and to the Holy Spirit,
As it was in the beginning, is now and ever shall be,
World without end. Amen

Sunday 8th April
Easter Sunday   John 20:1–9

Early on the first day of the week, while it was still dark, Mary Magdalene came to the tomb and saw that the stone had been removed from the tomb. So she ran and went to Simon Peter and the other disciple, the one whom Jesus loved, and said to them, "They have taken the Lord out of the tomb, and we do not know where they have laid him." Then Peter and the other disciple set out and went toward the tomb. The two were running together, but the other disciple outran Peter and reached the tomb first. He bent down to look in and saw the linen wrappings lying there, but he did not go in. Then Simon Peter came, following him, and went into the tomb. He saw the linen wrappings lying there, and the cloth that had been on Jesus' head, not lying with the linen wrappings but rolled up in a place by itself.

Then the other disciple, who reached the tomb first, also went in, and he saw and believed; for as yet they did not understand the scripture, that he must rise from the dead.

- Can I imagine myself standing near to the tomb on the morning in question, before first light? I observe the comings and goings.

- How do the people look? First, the woman; can I see her face? What does she do next? Then two men. . . .

- What has happened here?

Coming this Fall
Sacred Space: The Prayer Book 2008

Sacred Space
The Prayer Book 2008
Jesuit Communication Centre, Ireland
Now in its fourth year, the 2008 edition of *Sacred Space: The Prayer Book* offers a practical, portable way to pray throughout the year. *Sacred Space* offers a daily scripture selection followed by points of inspiration to help you consider the passage and its relevance to daily life. The book also provides weekly themes, and you are encouraged to reflect everyday on the six stages of prayer specifically created for the theme of the week.
384 pages / $14.95

ave maria press

Available from your bookstore or from
ave maria press / Notre Dame, IN 46556
www.avemariapress.com / Ph: 800-282-1865
A Ministry of the Indiana Province of Holy Cross

Keycode: F0A0107000